I'LL HOLD YOU IN HEAVEN

I'LL HOLD YOU IN HEAVEN

HEALING AND HOPE FOR THE
PARENT WHO HAS LOST A CHILD
*through Miscarriage, Stillbirth
Abortion or Early Infant Death*

Jack Hayford

Regal Books
A Division of Gospel Light
Ventura, California, U.S.A.

Published by Regal Books
A Division of GL Publications
Ventura, California U.S.A.
Printed in U.S.A.

The essential substance of this book first published in the Living Way
paperback *Early Flight*—© 1986.

Library of Congress Cataloging-in-Publication Data
Hayford, Jack W.
I'll hold you in heaven : healing and hope for the parent of a miscar-
ried, aborted, or stillborn child / Jack W. Hayford.

            p.   cm.
   Rev. ed. of: Early flight. 1986.
   ISBN 0-8307-1459-6
   1. Consolation. 2. Children—Death—Religious aspects—Chris-
tianity. 3. Miscarriage. 4. Still-birth. 5. Abortion—Religious aspects—
Christianity. I. Hayford, Jack W. Early flight. II. Title.
BV4907.H38 1990
248.8'6—dc20
                                90-44573
                                     CIP

8 9 10 11 12 13 14 15 16 / KP / X3 / 99 98 97 96 95 94 93

Rights for publishing this book in other languages are contracted by Gospel Lit-
erature International (GLINT). GLINT also provides technical help for the adap-
tation, translation and publishing of Bible study resources and books in scores
of languages worldwide. For further information, contact GLINT, P.O. Box
4060, Ontario, CA 91761-1003, U.S.A., or the publisher.

Table of Contents

Introduction

The Spirit of the Lord is upon
Me, because He has...sent Me
to heal the brokenhearted.

—Luke 4:18

As a pastor, a shepherd of souls, I find myself, time and time again, meeting people who have suffered the death of a baby, either before or shortly after birth. If you have experienced the great crisis to which I refer, it's quite possible that you are searching for something—anything—powerful enough to calm the questions that may rage inside your heart.

You may be among the great number of women and men who have planned, prepared and prayed for a child—but the baby was stillborn, dead on arrival. Perhaps you are one of the thousands of parents whose newborn babies lived so short a life as to have hardly, truly arrived; babies who died a few hours, days or weeks after birth. Together, parents of the stillborn and of the newly born who die form a distinct group of people who had a baby they never got to keep.

Or maybe you are the parent of a child lost to abortion. If so, you may be like so many others that I meet, suffering greatly in the aftermath of the procedure proponents hail as so "prompt" and "painless." Untold numbers of women and men are stumbling through the emotional carnage following an abortion—some believing their decision was wrong, others racked with uncertainty. The pain runs deep.

Finally, you may belong to a third group of the disappointed: the hosts of women who longed for a child, but two or three—four or maybe five—months into their pregnancy something went awry and they miscarried.

If you have experienced the wrenching loss of a child in the womb or during the weeks and months following birth, you are hardly alone. The parents of the stillborn or the newly born who die; the miscarrying mother and the maternal victim of abortion, are all parents of children who were designed for a lifetime of purpose; children whose lives were cut short.

In the Creator's finest plan, these children were not intended for the disease, death or destruction that took their lives. Yet they died. Like a rescheduled airplane suddenly departing ahead of time, these took an "early flight." Before we could ever know them—their possibilities, their presence and purpose—they were gone. Whether their hastened departure was forced through accident, neglect or abuse of the fetus...whether through disease, deformity or simple malfunction...suddenly they departed.

For those who remain at the airport of the present, there can be tears, pain, bitterness and questions—but I assure you that there is also hope.

In recent years, as I encountered increasing

numbers of hurting people whose parenthood had been cut short, I began to search God's Word to seek a case for *hope*. I wanted to find truth that could heal and give comfort in the midst of the pain following the amputation of a life from its present potential.

And thus, the pages of this book. In the following chapters you will find scripturally-based answers to many of the questions you may have found yourself asking: At the time of your miscarriage or abortion, did your baby have a soul? And what about the stillborn child, or the baby who dies shortly after birth? Is he or she in heaven? If so, what is he or she like, this child who never developed character or personality beyond the womb? Will you ever see your child again? And how will you recognize your child when you finally meet in heaven?

The purpose of this book is to offer a path to hope and healing—not through "happy talk" or platitudes, but through the solid footing of the holy truth of God's Word. The biblical foundation for hope and comfort is strong; the Scriptures indeed offer a way out of the depths of grief.

If you have experienced the loss of a child through the tragedy of abortion, God's Word offers you something more; it offers forgiveness and healing for the series of choices that led you into the abortionist's chamber. Abortion is not only a tough topic, but a delicate one. And it's a tragedy. But my object in these pages is not to elaborate that tragedy or underscore the facts of human failure. Rather, I seek to offer comfort and direction for the future.

There was a time when I was not unlike many Christians, wrestling against bitterness, self-righteousness and even condemnation toward the parents of aborted children. I was not only angry that lives were being taken, but I felt superior. And that was the hateful blindness I had to deal with; the cocksureness of my self-righteous opinion.

In that state I couldn't even begin to gain perspective on the fear, pain, hurt, agony and embarrassment of so many who needed something else from me. Society has so liberalized abortion that the uninformed and uncounseled readily give in, until, in the aftermath of the experience, the living victims bend beneath another burden—the burden of questions: "What have I done?" "Who might the child have become?" "Was I right? Wrong? Can I ever forget?" "What would have happened if I hadn't...?"

Meeting increasing numbers of women and men who ache over the ramifications of their "right to choose" has not changed my convictions about the wrongness of abortion, but it has cured my soul of the wrongness of my superficial point of view. I now see a place where life, light and love are desperately needed—a place in our world where truth not only can shine like a beacon light discerning good and evil, but where that same truth can also shed the light of healing, warmth and hopefulness. If you are, indeed, one of the many adult victims of abortion, then read on. You are on the verge of the discovery of forgiveness, healing and hope.

It is to any parent who remembers—with tears, pain, bitterness or questions—a stillborn, miscarried, aborted or early-dead child that I dedicate these moments in God's Word. And for those among us who have never known such pain, failure or grief, my hope is that an enlargement of heart may occur. May God's Spirit speaking His Word create a new space within *all* of us, making a place where we can host with understanding and compassion all those we know or will meet who have been left with aching heart and empty arms following a little one's early flight from this life.

So, come with me to the fountain of truth—to God's Word—where eternal wisdom, reconciling righteousness and healing hope abound. Let's find out what we can about God's answers to one of the most wrenching traumas in our present society: the pain following the too-early death of an infant.

1
The Gift of Lives

And the Lord God formed
man of the dust of the ground,
and breathed into his nostrils
the breath of life; and man
became a living being.

—Genesis 2:7

THE FOUNDATIONS OF HOPE AMID ANY HUMAN dilemma, or in fact of any human disobedience, will always be drawn from God's Word—not from human reasoning or happy-talk philosophizing. The answer to your deepest pain or most grieving heart cry lies in Scripture. What then, should be your first question?

Perhaps the best place to begin is with the simple query: Was my yet unborn child, in the fullest sense of the word, actually a human being? That question must be settled with confidence and personal certainty. God's answer gives rise to an amazing basis for hope—an expectancy never before anticipated as possible. So let's discover what the Creator Himself has to say on the subject.

Our first objective is to establish a biblical basis for the prenatal existence of the human soul. Is a person a person before they are born?

Here is the crux of the matter. For if we are only dealing with chemistry or tissue, in examining the nature of the fetus or the stillborn, there is little at stake. But in most of us, an inner monitor signals that there is something more involved here than mere chemical combinations or complex structures of tissues. Could it be that God has given a conclusive and confirming witness in His Word, to companion with that internal sense most everyone shares—that sense that the life of an embryo is eternal?

Without surrendering to either mystery or superstition, we can assertively say, yes! The life of the child in the womb *is* eternal. But please be clear: This is a statement born from far more than either religious opinion, occult dogma, or human imagination.

The religionist may trumpet the *reality* of, and therefore the sanctity of life in the womb. But so often these assertions lead to the leveling of accusations. Too easily the focus falls solely on the sin of life's sanctity having been violated, and the hearer rebels. Even if the call to protect life 's worthy, it is a false victory to suppose that proclamation is more important than the good news of God's grace, love and healing forgiveness. Life is sacred, to be sure. But many need to see sacred truth that extends beyond that fact; truth which offers other facts after human blindness may have overlooked that first fact of life's sanctity.

On another front, the reincarnationist proposes that all human life is merely the recycling of personalities in new bodies, with hopes on ever-improving one's lot in life with each recycling experience. But whatever the wish, hope or pretended logic of such a proposition, honesty requires that we immediately dispense with those notions. God's Word abolishes the phantom philosophies of reincarnation. According to the final revelation of the Bible, life is a one-time proposition for each of us insofar as this world is concerned. Life is an appointment that (1) has God's divine purpose, and (2) requires our accountability:

"It is appointed unto man to live and die but once—after this comes his evaluation before God."[1] Contrary to the confused ideas of a few sincere souls, Jesus' words, "You must be born again," do not have anything whatsoever to do with another birth beyond this lifetime. Being "born again" is clearly explained by Jesus Himself. He clarified new birth as an internal renewal, and He specified our need to experience it in *this* lifetime to do so by welcoming Him into our life as Savior and Lord.[2]

Another realm of error distills from the poetic notion that, while not a recycled personality having lived life before, each baby had existence prior to the womb. This scenario somehow envisions God as a heavenly Father doling out angel-spirits across the earth: installing them in baby-bodies either before or at birth. This unscriptural and insensitive idea is at the root of the frequently parroted statement, so sincerely spoken at the funerals of young children, that God somehow "knew better" and that He "took back" the life He had earlier given from heaven.

However well-intended the thought, God didn't and doesn't "take babies because He needs them in heaven." The pain and problem of death exists on this planet because humanity has broken its trust with the treasure of life. And the Bible doesn't say anything at all about God making independent decisions about the placement of each life into each body. Let's see what it does say.

When God "Breathes"

Genesis 2 elaborates what chapter 1 introduces: God, having created man, told him to be fruitful and multiply. Now the Word of God relates how man's possibilities and capabilities for this "multiplying" were given by his Creator. They are summarized in these words:

> *And the Lord God formed man of the dust of the ground, and breathed into his nostrils the breath of life; and man became a living being.*[3]

Literally, the Hebrew text reads that God, in creating the father and motner of the race, placed *in them* the capacity to beget life: He "breathed" into them—the breath of *chayeem* —that is, *lives*. Notice closely the plural of the word for *life*: God gave mankind the gift of *lives*. The concept transcends the obvious Creator-gift of life for each one to *experience*, and reaches further to the gift of *lives* placed within each one's capacity to *beget*.

That one phrase—that God breathed into man *lives*—clearly reveals how God has endowed mankind with *both* (1) the *capacity* to beget life and (2) the *responsibility* to do so. The ramifications of this fact are profound.

First, this ability has been placed at man's discretion. Each time the conception of a child occurs, God does *not* have to take separate action to infuse the fertilized ovum with life. Life is simply *inherently present*—instantly, spontaneously, always *there*, because God delegated "lives" to man for propagation. The awesome ability to reproduce eternal *souls* as well as physical *bodies* has been given to mankind.

Second, until that union of sperm and egg occurs, we as individual men and women are the stewards of that life-begetting potential. No given number of off-spring is mandated by God to any of us. God never indicates a requirement as to quantity, but only that there be a will to say yes—that we *will* have children, in obedience to His command, "Be fruitful...multiply."[4]

Contrary to the thinking of some sincere people, the Bible does *not* say birth control is wrong. God has given each of us—mankind—the responsibility of governing the *multiplication* of life. While He *has* commanded him to *beget* children, He has *not* mandated an interminable abandonment to chance, *or* required a given number of offspring; or assigned us to *in*numerable ones!

What the Bible *does* say, however, is that children are a blessing and should be *sought:*

> *Behold, children are a heritage from*
> *the Lord,*
> *The fruit of the womb is His reward.*[5]

The Word of God employs the loveliest terminology in describing the joy of childbirth, the meaningfulness of parenthood and the desirability of a family. But the Bible further implies that since life begins at conception, the willful extinguishing of that life is *not* an acceptable method of birth control. According to God's Word the frequency of conception *can* be controlled, but life once conceived cannot be taken at human will. In short, (1) *man is not* to completely avoid begetting children; (2) nor is he to abort those who have been conceived.

So, we see from the very establishing of the creative order:

- God has placed life immediately within man's capacity to reproduce;
- He has called him to exercise that life-begetting capacity; and
- He clearly expects that once life is conceived, its preciousness be honored.

We do not need to go to the laboratory to see if life begins at conception, nor are we at the mercy of volatile emotions on the subject. Rather the cool, crisp words of God's timeless truth show us created man, who from his beginning has possessed the God-given ability to beget another being created like himself. This kind of life is in the loins of *both* the man and the woman when each contributes his share toward the multiplication process, and in the instant those cells conjoin, another life begins.

NOTES

1. Hebrews 9:27, (author's paraphrase)
2. See John 3:1-12
3. Genesis 2:7
4. Genesis 1:28
5. Psalm 127:3

2
When Does Significance Begin?

God obviously anticipated our inquiry centuries ahead of time.

NOT ONLY DOES THE BIBLE ESTABLISH THE FACT of the prenatal existence of your child as a human being, it further teaches the worth, importance and spiritual viability of every pre-born life. David observed how true this is in praising God for how He takes note of and protects the fetus.

> *For You [Lord] have formed my inward parts; You have covered me in my mother's womb.*[1]

This text makes direct reference to the deepest part of our being—the "inward parts." The Hebrew term *kilyaw* was the figurative expression used in that language to represent the "foundation of being." Just as we refer to the "heart" as the seat of our being or inner person, the Hebrew tongue referred to the kidneys *(kilyaw)*. The use in the Scriptures of this expression, referring to a child in the womb, unquestionably establishes biblical support for the idea that a *spiritual* "being," not only a physical one, *does* exist in the womb.

And notice how God's personal attentiveness toward each fetus is so beautifully declared: "You covered me," David announces; that is, "You came to my help." A close scrutiny of the verb chosen by Jewish translators of this passage reveals that the literal statement of the

text is that God is *beside* the child—to *help* it
and to *keep* it from its earliest beginning.[2]

One can't help but wonder to what David
might have been referring. As a child, had his
mother told him stories of her being especially
protected—sustained by God's intervening
grace during her pregnancy? Might David be
saying that he was spared by some providence,
or is he simply making a general statement
about God's care for the child in the womb? In
any case, the inescapable truth is that His personal attention is declared; Jesus strongly
affirmed God's personal concern for each individual; noting His very real Creator-care for a
mere sparrow, and then saying God's care was
multiplied times *more* for each child, each person, each human being.[3] The whole of Psalm
139 gives us a mighty insight: God views life in
the womb as (1) real and eternal; and shows
us (2) it is desirable and worth protecting.

When in the Womb Does Valid Life Begin?

This question has captured the interest of
philosophers and scientists over the centuries,
as man has sought to define exactly when life
actually begins. More recently, debate has cen-
tered on the question as to which trimester—
that is, which three-month segment of the nine

months of pregnancy—life may in fact become "human."

It seems that God anticipated this specific question ages ago, for in the Bible we have a case in which the most precise evidence is given, showing us that *viable, significant* life in the womb specifically exists during *all* of the first three months; that is, *from conception fully meaningful life* is present.

Of course, the biologist has shown the poignant physiological evidences of life in the first three months: The third week, the lobes of the brain are distinguishable; the fourth week, the head and face are recognizable and the heart starts to beat; during weeks five and six, the eyes are identifiable and legs are putting on flesh and muscle; in the eighth week the embryo moves to the fetal stage and the following weeks, sex can be identified; the baby can begin to turn its head, squint, frown, make a fist and even get the hiccups: all of this is *before* the end of the first three months in the womb![4]

But as touching as these biological signs of humanity are in the *physical* formation of the babe-in-the-womb, look with me at the pointed evidence the Bible gives of the *personal, spiritual* viability of that child. An unmistakable statement is present here, as God has placed at the heart of His Word a story which reveals the fact of a baby's real, personal meaning-filled existence during the first three months following conception. It's the story that is among the best known of all in the world. Although given to tell us of the gift of our Redeemer, hidden within this story is a precious fact concerning the Creator's basic gift of life itself.

Mary, the young woman of Nazareth, has received an angelic visitation announcing her role as the mother of the Messiah. We pick up the story in Luke, chapter 1:

> *Now Mary arose in those days and went into the hill country with haste, to a city of Judah, and entered the house of Zacharias and greeted Elizabeth. And it happened, when Elizabeth heard the greeting of Mary, that the babe leaped in her womb; and Elizabeth was filled with the Holy Spirit. Then she spoke out with a loud voice and said, "Blessed are you among women, and blessed is the fruit of your womb! But why is this granted to me, that the mother of my Lord should come to me?"* [5]

The words of Mary's cousin Elizabeth are astonishingly relevant to the philosophical inquiry of this twentieth century. The precision of the text seems crafted by the Holy Spirit twenty centuries in advance. Within the span of 30 verses in Luke's Gospel (1:26-56), we are explicitly told:

- A child has been conceived in Mary's womb;
- It is spoken of as present, as alive, and as "the Lord" at the moment—no less a person for being a fetus; and
- The exact chronology of the event.

In verse 36, the angel told Mary at the same time as *her* conception, that Elizabeth was in her sixth month of pregnancy. In verse 56, we are told Mary stayed with her until the birth of Elizabeth's baby—"*And Mary remained with her about three months.*" In other words, when Elizabeth was filled with the Holy Spirit and prophesied upon Mary's arrival—"the child in your womb is the Lord"—Mary was only a matter of a few days into *her* pregnancy.

It's astounding.

It's a prophetic statement cut from the cloth of human experience two millennia ago and unrolled before mankind today. Does the Bible say that life in its truest essence exists from conception?

Absolutely!

Does it specifically answer questions about the first trimester of pregnancy?

Absolutely!

And the most profound revelation to the thoughtful reader and inquirer should be *not* in the fact the question is answered, but in the manifest fact that God obviously anticipated our inquiry centuries ahead of time. The meticulous detail, written without strain to the natural flow of the story, silences the doubts of any who accept the authority of God's Holy Word: Life—personal life, meaningful life, *human* life in its deepest, lasting sense—exists in the womb from conception. We are not only shown the evidences of a real body in formation during the first trimester, but we are given a conclusive statement concerning a real *being* at the same time: a *human*—a lasting, eternal soul—is present from conception.

The Point Is Permanence

And what is the point of this exercise in Bible exegesis?

Simply this: To establish a foundation for the *permanent* existence of the child you lost through stillbirth, miscarriage, abortion or infant death.

Your child *still* exists! It not only *was* a real, valid, meaningful person from the instant of its conception, but it has *continued* to be a real, lasting, eternal being since the moment of its death.

- The miscarried child did not disappear as a being simply because a clump of tissue slipped from its grip in the womb.
- The aborted baby did not cease its larger existence simply because a surgical instrument or vacuum scraped or sucked its physical existence into oblivion.
- And to the parent of the stillborn, or to those who have held a dead baby in their arms—one who died so shortly after birth, seeming to have flown before it was truly known, caught away by an early flight—I tell you, that child's soul (and the same with the miscarried and aborted) is no less caught up to God's presence as an eternal being than the soul of a ninety-year old man or woman, dying and going to their Maker.

The Word of God, the Creator's "handbook for humanity," gives us understanding at this initial point of inquiry: What about the reality of life of the blastula, the embryo, the fetus, the stillborn? His answer: *it's real.* And therein a biblical point of hope is present, for this means that your lost child is in God's presence, and you will someday meet him or her.

For Some, a Dilemma

But I can almost hear someone asking, "What

if the child I will someday meet in heaven is one that I made a choice to abort? Will he accuse me of disallowing him life as I have been allowed it?"

What a poignant question.

What a potentially haunting specter: to arrive in the afterworld, to stand in the presence of God and to be indicted *not* only by the Almighty Himself, but by a being never really known, yet in that moment completely recognized. How unimaginable, to have that person rise, pointing to you, and say, "That is the one who bore me...and the one who denied me life on earth." What a stark, raw, emotion-shattering scene! Could such a moment be?

On the ground of God's Word, the answer is NEVER!

NEVER!

Any judgment before God's throne will be declared by Him alone. He will not marshall witnesses against us, for it is solely with Him we have to deal when we give our accounting, and He is the faithful witness of all our lives.[6]

Furthermore, the fear of recrimination for ANY sin or failure NEVER needs to cloud your soul, because the largest fact in the universe is the fact of God's provision for *all* of our forgiveness:

> *For God so loved the world that He gave His only begotten Son, that whoever believes in Him should not perish but have everlasting life.*[7]

And your or my relative undeservedness of such merciful love and great forgiveness is not an obstacle:

> *For God demonstrates His own love to us, in that while we were still sinners, Christ died for us.*[8]

The happy and holy consequence of Christ's death for our sins is that complete payment has been made and complete forgiveness is fully available to you and me today.

I run a very real risk by examining, in this manner, the heartache of abortion and the path to healing. It is entirely possible that someone may misjudge my desire to comfort, concluding that correction is needed instead. But my effort is not prompted by a casual attitude toward the fact that fetuses are being killed. Instead, I am driven by the realization that most mothers who choose abortion are not indifferent to the child within. If the memory of an abortion lurks in your past, your choice was promoted and encouraged by a society temporarily numbed to the truest values of human life. And while this societal influence does not lessen the magnitude of your personal choice, let me ask you this: Which one of us is free from the ramifications and pain inflicted by our own sinful choices? The glimmering hope of one and all is that Jesus Himself reaches in tenderness to each of us in the aftermath of our own hurtful decisions; that Jesus Himself brings good news to broken people.

Let me ask you something—and it's not merely if you've felt shame, guilt or stain by your part in the sadness of an abortion. Indeed, even if abortion is not one of the failures in your past, every one of us has sinned. Total honesty before God brings with it a sense of condemnation for choices in our pasts, as well as factors still very much a part of the present. Is this how you feel? Is there something in your past or in your present that cries out to be admitted and abandoned, confessed, cleansed and forgiven?

Listen. There's good news today.

God's provisions for our past are not only sufficient, but His promise for our future is incredibly bright! A brilliant light shines from the face of Jesus, not only burning away the darkness of sin-shadows which seek to engulf the soul, but radiating a beam of brightness into the future.

Open your heart to Him—to His love, hope and comfort: *"For as many as received Him, to them He gives the right to become children of God."*[9] If you've never asked forgiveness for past sin, *of any* or *every* kind; or if you've never invited our Savior Jesus Christ to enter your life in healing love and saving power, do it now.

Prayerfully bow and speak your heart cry to Him.

And having done so, in the spirit of peace which His healing truth and love can bring, questions about those little ones who have taken the early flight are answered by a new level of hope, elevated by the fact that your soul has had its greatest need supplied:

A Savior.

If you have never personally welcomed the Lord Jesus into your heart, to be *your* Savior and to lead you in the matters of *your* life, I would like to encourage and help you to do that.

There is no need to delay, for an honest heart can approach the loving Father God at any time. So I'd like to invite you to come with me and let's pray to Him right now.

If it's possible there where you are, bow your head—or even kneel, if you can. But in either case, let me pray a simple prayer first— then, I've added words for you to pray yourself:

My prayer:

"Father God, I have the privilege of joining with this child of Yours who is reading this book right now. I want to thank You for the openness of heart being shown toward You, and I want to praise You for Your promise, that when we call to You, You will answer.

"I know that genuine sincerity is present in this heart, which is ready to speak this prayer, and so we come to You in the name and through the Cross of Your Son, the Lord Jesus. Thank You for hearing." (And now, you speak your prayer.)

Your prayer:

"Dear God, I am doing this because I believe in Your love for me, and I want to ask You to come to me as I come to You. Please help me now.

"First, I thank You for sending Your Son Jesus to earth to live and to die for me on the Cross. I thank You for the gift of forgiveness of sin that You offer me now, and I pray for that forgiveness.

"Do, I pray, forgive me and cleanse my life in Your sight, through the blood of Jesus Christ. I am sorry for anything and everything I have ever done that is unworthy in Your sight. Please take away all guilt and shame, as I accept the fact that Jesus died to pay for all my sins, and through Him I am now given forgiveness on this earth and eternal life in heaven.

"I ask You, Lord Jesus, please come into my life *now*. Because You rose from the dead, I know You're alive and I want You to live with me—now and forever.

"I am turning my life over to You, and turning from my way to Yours. I invite Your Holy Spirit to fill me and lead me forward in a life that will please the heavenly Father.

"Thank You for hearing me. From this day forward, I commit myself to Jesus Christ the Son of God. In His Name, Amen."

If you have received Jesus Christ as your Savior, it would be my pleasure to send you a gift copy of my book on how a newborn believer in Christ can grow. Please remove the last printed page in this book, fill in the address information, and mail to me. Your decision will be held in confidence; we will pray for you; and you will be sent a copy of NEWBORN: Your New Life with Christ *(Tyndale House Publishers).*

NOTES

1. Psalm 139:13
2. Septuagint: *antilambano*
3. Matthew 10:31
4. Source: *LIFE* magazine reprint, copyright 1965, 1979.
5. Luke 1:39-43
6. Hebrews 4:13; 2 Corinthians 5:10
7. John 3:16
8. Romans 5:8
9. See John 1:12

3
Life to What Degree?

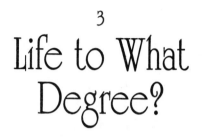

Our investigation of such
questions must be more than
merely theoretical or theological,
and in making the Creator's
Handbook our textbook, we
have substance, not theory.

I N THE LIGHT OF GOD'S ETERNAL WORD, WE HAVE established the fact that life does indeed begin at conception; that even before birth a fully significant being has begun its realization of the Creator's purpose for its own self.

In discussing the aborted, miscarried or stillborn, another question rises:

>*Since* the body never reaches completion, as with the miscarried or aborted:

>*Since* it never grows beyond birth, as with the stillborn;

>*Since* those lips never cried, much less spoke intelligibly;

>*Since* that tininess hardly thought reflectively...or made a self-conscious assessment of its own being; then,

>*what is the exact nature of that undeveloped "eternal being"?*

The popular consensus would be that your child never was, or if it "was" somehow, no longer *is*. The natural deduction of the mind unenlightened by divine revelation is that the infant-life so sadly wasted, either by physical malfunction or decisive human intervention, could never realize a destiny—indeed, probably never had one. But just as ignorance forfeits hope, insight can regain it.

We have already found that each child has, before birth, a divinely ordained endlessness to its being: Humankind once conceived become eternal souls, since life does not begin with their first breath or the first heartbeat. It begins at once with the initial uniting of the cells contributed by the mother and father. From that moment according to the Bible, a viable being exists; a being which transcends its relative physical durability—be it eight hours within the womb or eighty years beyond it.

This being God's conclusive word on the subject, we may logically ask: Then what is the eternal destiny of the unborn, stillborn or early-death child? If the child never knew a life on earth, what becomes of it? What purpose? What intelligence has it? Indeed, it may be eternal, but an eternal "what"? To what degree does this life exist?

Grounds for Understanding

Our investigation of such questions must be more than merely theoretical or theological, and in making the Creator's Handbook our textbook, we have substance, not theory. We are not guessing, for God's Word of truth eliminates guesswork. Neither are we theologizing for the sake of academic argument. God didn't give His Word as a text for forming ritual creeds but as a source for answering human need.

Our foremost need is to know God's love and forgiveness, but with this we also need the hope He extends. Only His Word offers the pathway to discovery of His purpose; a functional purpose that brings both meaning to our lives and strength to rise beyond our weaknesses. God has given insights in His Word that can counter our doubts and conquer our fears, bringing lasting hope that our failures or disappointments need not preempt our possibilities.

This is what God's program of redemption is about: The restoration of life *and hope*.

Redemption has a triple focus, but the middle one is so often blurred. Part I—God redeems our past and Part III promises us eternal joy in heaven. But Part II, which says He provides hope and power for our present experiences, offering a beautiful and fulfilling life *now*, is too often not understood. He forgives us to give us a future, and He redeems us to begin a program of restoring all that we have lost, whether through our helplessness, ignorance, neglect, failure or sin.

Thus, with direct reference to the subject of the destiny of those little ones who have taken early flight from this world, we have reason for great expectation. Examination of the solid ground of the Scriptures gives footing for faith in a future beyond our heartaches. To determine exactly what your "early flight" child may be or become beyond the womb, we must answer these questions:

- Is that being—your child—sensitive and responsive as a spiritual entity? Is there evidence that it possesses insight or "intellect" in the most spiritual sense of the word?
- If so, is there a positive eternal destiny ensured for these children we never knew? What of heaven? Where in heaven? Or, heaven at all?

The Bible is anything but silent about the spiritual nature of these little ones and yet I had never heard any teaching concerning these questions. I confess, I would never have begun this quest to probe these passages were it not for two factors.

First, as pastor of a large, growing urban congregation, I was repeatedly encountering believers, newly born again to faith in Jesus Christ, whose past contained the pain of memories related to abortion. They wondered about the life of the one they had extinguished from this planet.

Second, an unusual and very interesting conversation took place. Let me tell you the story.

My wife, Anna, and I were talking with an older lady one day; a dear saint who had been part of our congregation. Over the years we had come to know her as both a sensitive and sensible person. Except for the fact that she was such a balanced, spiritually-minded, scripturally-ordered person, we probably would not have been ready to put much stock in the episode she related. In a nonmystical, very natural and unaffected way, she recounted the following:

"Shortly after my husband and I had our first child, almost immediately I became pregnant again. Because we were so young, because it was during the Depression and because neither of us knew Christ nor God's Word of promise, we sought and I experienced an abortion. Some years later, after our other children were fully grown, I was at prayer one day—not even thinking of this long-past fact of our lives—when the Holy Spirit said: 'You have never presented that child to the Father.' I was quite taken back, not because I felt shamed or condemned, but because I hadn't even been thinking about that abortion experience. Second, it would *never* have occurred to me to *ever* make an actual dedication of an aborted child to God.

"Still, the experience being so clear, I spoke with my husband about it, and after prayer and studying the Word of God, we did exactly that—we dedicated our child together. We knew we had long since been forgiven for the sin we shared at that time, in our ignorance of God's better way. But now we simply prayed: 'Lord, You are the Father of all spirits. Your Word says so, and we believe You not only gave us an eternal soul whose body we mistreated in our ignorance, but whose being still exists within Your great domain. Knowing nothing more, we humbly come to present this child You gave us—to present it to You. And we do this in Jesus' Name. Amen.'"

Now, that couple did *not* feel that prayer was accomplishing some "salvation-by-proxy" or any such foolish notion. Nor were they presenting a new doctrine or some pattern of behavior they felt should be observed by everyone who shared their particular failure. To the contrary, they simply were responding to something they felt within their own hearts. That act of dedication was not so much for the baby's benefit as for their own, for the experience helped them to a genuine realization of the fact that their baby still exists—

something they had not considered as deeply before.

As for me, it was the hearing of that episode that finally prodded me into a diligent study of the Scriptures. As a result, I was not only moved, edified and enlightened by the Word as I pursued this theme for teaching the congregation, but since then I have shared these truths with countless numbers via the media.

A Glimpse from Jeremiah

Now we come to the question of the *spiritual* capacity of the unborn child. Begin with me at the words of the prophet Jeremiah.

> *Before I formed you in the womb I knew you; before you were born I sanctified you.*[1]

Although it is clear in the text that Jeremiah is specifically speaking about God's Word to him personally, the Bible is equally clear that God is no respecter of persons. He is as committed to *each* of us as He is to *any* of us, and it is in that understanding our glimpse from Jeremiah becomes a look at God's view of each of us—while we were yet unborn.

The prophet pointedly attests to God's revelation that man's prenatal existence is linked to a postnatal one; in other words, the life of our soul is an eternal, spiritual continuum that begins at conception and continues through and beyond birth. Just as our bodies experience a *temporal* physical continuum that begins in the womb and continues to grow and function beyond it for our *earthly* lifetime, so our spirits—the essence of our life—exist from conception and beyond for our *eternal* lifetime.

While notably underscoring the ongoing spiritual viability of the child who never experiences life outside the womb, this verse yields two giant facts about *every* human: the *first* reveals divine intent, or purpose; the *second* reveals divine input, or provision.

Intent and Purpose

The words, *"Before I formed you in the womb I knew you,"* do not suggest the preexistence of the personality but they do teach God's pre-awareness of and intent for the child. He is saying for each of us to understand, "None of you is an accident. I have foreknown your conception. I have preplanned and provided purpose for your life." To personally apply the essence of this concept can be mightily transforming for any of us.

In private counsel I have met so many people whose sense of personal worth was repeatedly demeaned during their childhood by such remarks as, "We never planned on you"; or "If we had known what we were doing we would have had fewer children." Such depersonalizing feelings are often accentuated when people discover they were illegitimate offspring or the product of some extramarital affair. Individuals question their worth, despair over their destiny, and often succumb to feelings of pointlessness—especially in a society that argues for *chance* as the explanation of man's creation rather than God's *purpose*.

But to all human fear, blindness, sin and misgiving, God speaks from His Word. He was not caught by surprise where *any* of us were concerned! "Before you were formed in the womb, I knew you." Let that deep statement of His primary intent and purpose for every human being seep into *your* soul, and let it be a hallmark of our awareness about each child in the womb. Whatever the frustration, inconvenience, pain or displeasure, there is no being without purpose in the larger providences of God. His purposes may not always harmonize with ours, but in the eternal symphony we will come to recognize better the part played by each creature—even when the note played by circumstances seems dissonant.

Input and Provision

Jeremiah 1:5 illustrates that God's purpose for people is already in force—in His mind and intent—while they are yet in the womb. "I have appointed you a prophet to the nations," God said of Jeremiah; and in respect to a planned purpose, he is not an exception, he is an example of God's intent. He is a proof case of the fact that no unborn child is without distinct spiritual significance in God's design.

But there is a second feature in this text, for in saying to Jeremiah, "I have appointed you a prophet," God is not merely making an assignment, He is ensuring a sufficiency. He assigns duty but He also gives the ability to accomplish it.

The implied message is that inherent in every child is not only the *promise* of God's purpose but the *provision* of God's power to accomplish the performance of that purpose. I feel particularly moved to point that out, because I have known of people tempted to abort a child through their unawareness of the dual truth this verse reveals. They not only haven't realized that God already has a *purpose* for the child, but they don't know God's *promise* of provision. Without hope or faith that He will provide for and help them see that child's purpose realized, fear and unbelief take over. I have even known of abortions performed simply because of fears of economic failure in the practical task of parenthood.

But God has a promise for such a person: If you'll let His purpose be realized in the child you may fear having, He'll help you at every point. Ask Him for wisdom and claim His promises to provide an adequate supply for material or monetary need. Ask and you will receive—and your joy in your children shall be full!

Spiritually Sensitive?

Is the unborn child a viable, real spiritual entity—a creature with God's purpose and power in beginning measure; a being with a sensitivity to the Almighty and His designs?

A classic case in evidence takes us back again to the Gospel of Luke, but this time to consider another baby, John the Baptist, who was yet in his mother Elizabeth's womb. The same passage we read earlier amplifies our understanding on yet another point.[2]

With the arrival of Mary, within whom the

Messiah Jesus had already been conceived, the child within Elizabeth is prompted to *leap*—literally jump in response to the present reality that was in the person of the yet unborn Christ. This is incredibly significant since, of John, an angel had prophesied to his father Zacharias, "He [John the Baptist] shall go before Him in the power of the Spirit [that is, before Messiah to announce His presence]." Amazingly, in fact it's almost humorous, the baby seems to be doing precisely that! What John would be doing with intelligent speech and by reason of spiritual cognizance 30 years later beside the Jordan River, he first does as an unborn child!

This is more than an interesting coincidence: The baby didn't just "happen" to jump. Rather, Elizabeth's own testimony attributes her certainty of God's witness to the occasion as being directly related to the baby's leaping within her. Man may call it superstition and we might be tempted to call it coincidental, but the Bible says it was the Holy Spirit at work.

Let no one say the unborn are without spiritual sensitivity or purpose. Intelligence may not have flowered as yet nor speech have been acquired, but a purpose has already been plotted by the Creator. The small human mass within the womb is already tuned to the Spirit of his or her Maker.

In Dr. Thomas Verney's book, *The Secret Life of the Unborn Child*, he notes the difference in the fetus's response, even as early as four and a half months, if either iodine or sugar is injected into the amniotic fluid of the womb. The child reacts disagreeably to the taste of iodine, but drinks at twice the normal rate of consumption if sugar is present. Verney goes on to say that unborn children react to the emotional charges they receive from the mother, noting that if the mother is really looking forward to a pregnancy, "it has an incredible, positive effect" on the baby.

We are unhesitant to acknowledge that the evidence is in as far as the natural realm is concerned. Let us be neither surprised to discover nor hesitant to acknowledge that the Bible tells us an unborn child is at least equally responsive and sensitive to the spiritual realm as well.

NOTES
1. Jeremiah 1:5
2. Luke 1:39-43

4
Destiny in the Afterworld

Man without a Savior is an eternally perishable being.

W E'VE ESTABLISHED THAT THE PRENATAL CHILD IS an eternal being capable of spiritual response. Now we ask, if a child dies before or shortly after birth, what is his or her destiny in the afterworld?

At once we open the question of options in the hereafter. Human philosophy suggests multiplied possibilities. God advises there are only two. Man's reasonings offer everything from oblivion to euphoria; from nothingness to anythingness; from extinction like a worm dried on the pavement, to an indeterminate number of incarnations as a being moves from one life to another. But God says once concluded on earth, human life proceeds to either heaven or hell.

No limbo.

No nirvana.

No purgatory.

No reincarnation.

No oblivion.

God's Word describes either (1) a destiny *within* His will and desire, or (2) a destiny resulting from *opposing* His will and desire. That these are the only options—eternal gain or eternal loss—is the only fact that gives credence to the extreme measure God's love required to ensure the possibility that each person can receive the promise of heaven.

> *God so loved the world that He gave His only begotten Son, that whoever believes in Him should not perish but have everlasting life.*[1]

Man without a Savior is an eternally perishable being. That "perishing" is *not* nothingness, but the endless suffering of a created soul separated from its Creator by its own choice and sin.

The apostle Paul elaborates the depth of this fact, accentuating again how the passion of Jesus Christ, who admittedly came and died essentially to rescue a truly lost humanity, verifies the reality and awfulness of the lostness of mankind.

> *For the love of Christ constrains us, because we judge thus: that if One died for all, then all died; and He died for all, that those who live should live no longer for themselves, but for Him who died for them and rose again.*[2]

The entire motive in Jesus Christ's coming was the love of our Creator who refuses to allow any of us—His own creation—to perish, without the availability of a way back from sin's self-initiated exile. God's goal is to bring us back, *into* the present fulfillment He offers and unto the eternal joy He created us to know.

With the fact of limited options in the after-world established in God's Word, what does He reveal concerning the disposition of the unborn or stillborn at their death?

To Heaven, or...?

Our hearts dictate "Heaven, of course!" And as true as that may well be, our answer must derive from greater authority than convictions born solely of our emotions. Doubtless we would all argue for their instantly being ushered into the Creator's heaven-home forever. And that answer *is* right, but we need grounds superior to our own human sense of justice. We need an authoritative statement from the Judge of the universe. What will He say?

With regard to these little ones, as with every human being coming before His presence at their passing, we can rest assured: *God is just.* He does not need any prompting from our emotional or rational proposals. Our insistence that "surely" or "of course" those unborn are "saved" is unnecessary here. God knows the spirit of the rebellious and that cosmic cul-de-sac called Hell is only a self-imposed place of endless abandonment for people who reject Him. Thus, unsurprisingly, His Word *is* clear concerning these sinless little ones: Their early departure from their short life here takes them immediately into His presence. And our hope can rest in that knowledge on the rock of His Word, not merely on our feelings.

God's Words on Dead Infants

Jesus' Words. It is with great tenderness that Jesus speaks of the innocence of little children: *"Their angels always see the face of My Father."* [3] His meaning is clearly that—notwithstanding every child's inherent potential for sinning— small children, yet in their innocence, still enjoy an uninterrupted discourse with the heart of God. At what age this is broken cannot be calendered, for it would vary with each person. Still, one thing is clear: An unborn or stillborn child hasn't transgressed that union.

David's Song. In the Old Testament David spoke of his departed son who died but days after birth: *"I shall go to him..."* [4] This statement is broadened in its significance when we note that it was spoken by the same lips which sang, *"and I will dwell in the house of the Lord forever."* [5] The place of eternal dwelling for the child now gone was known to be the same place anticipated by the believer who has received God's promise and redemption.

Abraham's Cry. When God told Abraham He was going to destroy Sodom and Gomorrah, Abraham asked, *"Will You also destroy the righteous with the wicked?"* He seems to be appealing to God in the interest of the innocent. Then, he apparently remembers that He doesn't need to goad God to do good, and at once he answers his own question, *"Far be it from You to do such a thing, to slay the righteous with the wicked, so that the righteous should be as the wicked; Far be it from You. Shall not the Judge of all the earth do right?"*[6]

Yes! A thousand times, Yes! The Judge of the Earth *can* be counted on *always*. He will do justice. He will do right. Always!

As with Abraham and with us and our children, God is fair on *heaven's* terms, not merely earth's. And in those eternal, abiding policies, the message of the Word teaches that the stillborn, the newly born who die, the miscarried and the aborted do indeed pass into the presence of God.

What About the Unsaved?

"But what if the parents are not believers?" Doesn't the Bible say something about the child then being outside God's grace as I have described?

This question is probably raised on the basis of a misunderstanding of 1 Corinthians 7:14: "For the unbelieving husband is sanctified by the wife, and the unbelieving wife is sanctified by the husband; otherwise your children are unclean, but now they are holy."

But this passage has nothing to do with the spiritual viability of the offspring of a spiritually mixed marriage, nor to do with the children of a couple neither of whom are saved.

In this text, the apostle Paul is addressing a moral question. The Corinthians were wondering about the legitimacy of children born to a couple where only one confessed Christ as Savior. Was their relationship impure, unholy—and thereby their children illegal or unsanctified in God's eyes? Paul's answer is swift and direct: "No, the children are in no way reduced in God's eyes"; they are declared socially and legally acceptable in God's sight. But in saying this, the Bible neither declares nor implies that parents determine the eternal destiny of their children. Believing couples do not automatically produce believing children, and conversely, the nonbelief of unbelieving parents does not automatically doom their children to eternal loss.

Salvation is always an individual choice. Parental influence during the child's lifetime does contribute very positively or negatively, but it cannot control it. As to the destiny of the unborn, since the children have made no moral choices, they have remained innocent. Thereby God's perfect justice receives them into His presence, irrespective of the spiritual condition of the parents—and without consideration of what the circumstance of the child's conception may have been.

In listening to all of this...

- Why does so much confusion, misunderstanding and condemnation surround us?
- Why do so many people wonder about purpose in their lives?
- Why does fear win over faith, and why are babies snuffed out in the womb like candles in the wind?
- Why does guilt successfully maintain its grip over so many in spite of the fact that God's forgiveness is so freely offered?
- Why does smallness of spirit compel believers to sit in judgment on human failure rather than to minister comfort and hope?

The answers to these questions are summarily handled, answered in their entirety in one direct statement which Jesus made:

> *The thief does not come except to steal, and to kill, and to destroy.*[7]

According to Christ, precisely what we are addressing is the work of the devil; a satanic *theft* of joy, a demonic *killing* of hope and a hellish *destruction* of lives. But the solution to mastery over our arch-opponent's workings is in Jesus' ensuing words:

> *I have come that they may have life, and that they may have it more abundantly.*[8]

Here is truth: the child of "early flight"—the stillborn, the newborn who dies, the miscarried, the aborted—is not a "nothing" that has gone nowhere.

- He or she was not just a small wad of cells washed down a drain. He or she was not just a mass of bones and tissue thrown into a plastic bag.
- He or she is not a stiffened corpse laid in a small coffin.

Rather, each of those little ones are present with the Father. They have identity, individuality and deserve to be known for what they are—eternal beings. They still have a divine purpose which, though it may transcend our understanding for the moment, we shall perceive clearly when the day dawns that we no longer see as through a glass, darkly, but then face-to-face.[9]

If comfort is what you need, I want to touch your hand. I want to pour the oil of hope into your heart if the flame has flickered and needs fuel to brighten tomorrow.

My friend, the truth can set you free—and the truth with which we deal is the Holy Spirit's key to your release. Whatever your heart calls for, whether remote to the immediate subject or directly in the center of it, let's call to Jesus Himself. He is the Truth incarnate and readily present. Invite His working into every facet of your present moment with your heartfelt prayer:

Come, Lord Jesus.

NOTES
1. John 3:16
2. 2 Corinthians 5:14,15
3. Matthew 18:10
4. 2 Samuel 12:23
5. Psalm 23:6
6. See Genesis 18:23-25
7. John 10:10
8. John 10:10
9. 1 Corinthians 13:12

5

In Heaven as a Person

Now there are heavenly bodies and there are earthly bodies and the glory of each is different from the other.

—1 Corinthians 15:40, paraphrase

To summarize, we have examined these truths from the Bible as they relate to your son or daughter lost through death:

- From conception, the life begun not only is truly human, but it is thereby truly an endless being. An eternal soul exists.
- Each unborn being has viable spiritual sensitivity. Although intellect and speech as we know it may not have begun, sensitivity, spiritual potential and distinctly human capacities are present.
- God places inestimable value on and has planned purpose for every human life, so much so that He gave His Son to recover from eternal loss all who will receive His redemption.
- The unborn, stillborn or infant at death does immediately pass into the presence of God—goes to heaven.

The sum of these statements is that the aborted, miscarried, stillborn or early-death child *exists*, it is with God as an eternal soul, and it is capable of spiritual, sensitive communication. But still another question reasonably comes to mind.

If the unborn child having died does actually go to heaven, in what form does it appear there? Since the child never developed beyond an embryo or fetus how would it appear in heaven? And even a stillborn child, though usually physically complete, generally has little distinct physical identification. How does it look in eternity?

Are such questions important?

I think so, because we are *all* creatures destined for eternity. Incorporated in God's presence in that eternal city will be all those beings who left before birth, as well as all of us who survived for a life span beyond it. We will meet one another there, and we will meet those infants. Once the horizons of that perspective open up, they may garner for each of us a host of biblically based values.

Here God's Word shines again as it so often does in the dark night of human pain. Consider what it says about a possible *meeting* with the child that left you before or shortly after birth.

A Meeting Someday

In the Old Testament, a marvelously tender story appears—a factual piece of history that climaxes a case of failure with a hope-filled promise.

You've heard the story.

From the balcony of his home, David sees

his neighbor Uriah's wife bathing. Filled with lust, he orders Bathsheba to his room and makes love to her, even while her warrior husband is away at battle, serving the very man who is taking his wife. The sordid details of the story result in Bathsheba's pregnancy, Uriah's murder and David's indictment by Nathan the prophet. "The child shall not live," Nathan declares.

Shortly after its birth, the baby begins to decline—death seems imminent. David seeks God's mercy with repentance, fasting and prayer; refusing food in order to intercede before God in behalf of the child.

When the child dies, David is not embittered, resentful nor any longer mournful. His servants are bewildered as he rises from prayer and ceases his mourning. And there, against that ancient backdrop of human ignorance about God's higher purposes for children who have died, David speaks the word of revelation—the word of God's truth. *"I shall go to him, but he shall not return to me."*[1]

Take special note of these words.

They are spoken by a man who sinned. Let us especially see how God-given hope springs in the breast of the very person who is in fact charged with being the *reason* the child didn't survive! But he is also a person who both lamented his failure and repented of it. And now he's speaking with hope: "I shall go to him."

David lived a long life following this episode, but here he is saying: "The day will come when I will meet that child, will greet that child, and I will some day forever be with that child."

That's in the Bible, friend. This isn't myth, fable, legend or a selection of poetic thoughts for the sorrowful. This is truth to set us free. Here you are specifically freed to expect to meet your child in heaven, to recognize him or her and to be with that child.

How Shall They Appear?

"But, Jack," I can almost hear somebody say, "what about the miscarried and aborted babies? How do they appear? How could I know or recognize them? In what form are they?"

Thankfully, the Word of God provides us with enough information that those are answerable questions, too. Although David was referring to a baby who died a few days after it was born, we can authoritatively answer concerning even a miscarried embryo, which may have been only weeks along the way toward birth.

From 1 Corinthians 15:40 we gain our first footing:

> *Now there are heavenly bodies and there are earthly bodies, and the glory of each is different from the other* (paraphrase).

The Bible makes two things clear; people who have departed earth's order of things are not wispy spooks, blowing in the wind. Satanic deceptions employ such ghostly projections and are practiced by occultists who conjure up horrifying demonic presences that delude, bind and purvey fear. But the few times we see people in the Bible who, to use the scriptural term, are in their "heavenly bodies," they are identifiable.

When the disciples on the Mount of Transfiguration saw Jesus talking with Moses and Elijah, they recognized them as human beings and intuitively knew who they were. They didn't witness double exposure-type pictures, nor were they struck dumb or horrified by ectoplasmic mirages. They saw *people* who had died. The Bible in fact distinctly mentions Moses' burial; and Elijah's experience, though unusual, did not preempt actual physical death. Of course, the disciples had never before seen Elijah and Moses and yet they knew immediately who they were.

"But how will I recognize someone who never had a body?"

This is more than a reasonable question. It is a difficult one. After all, if the miscarried or aborted child was not even completely formed at the time of its passing, what is there to meet...to greet?

God's Record of Your Appearance

Psalm 139 is an ode to the wonder of God's genius and love in providing us with the incredibly marvelous equipment we call the human body. In verses 15 and 16, the psalmist writes, *"My frame was not hidden from You, when I was made in secret, and skillfully wrought in the lowest parts of the earth. Your eyes saw my substance, being yet unformed. And in Your book they all were written, the days fashioned for me, when as yet there was none of them."*

Here, 30 centuries ago, is fantastic advance notice of something we have only begun to understand in this century. The writer is saying, "Lord, all my members are written in your book...even while they are yet being formed in the womb, You already have a record of what I shall physically become." *The New English Bible* puts it with this crystal clarity: *"Thou didst see my limbs unformed in the womb, and in thy book they are all recorded; day by day they were fashioned, not one of them was late in growing."* [2]

What "book" is that to which the Bible refers? Where is the book that lists the details of each one of our body's personal design and detailed development?

As recently as the 1950s, two biologists won the Nobel Prize upon discovering the secret of DNA, the spiralling double helix within the cellular structure of the human body that holds in coded form the details of every aspect of each person's physical potential. What's remarkable is this "book," so to speak, is within every *cell*—the *whole* blueprint. This means, essentially, that even in the smallest collection of cells formulating the tissue of a miscarried child, the encoded message of its physical development and appearance-to-be are already present. In short, God knows what your baby who wasn't born would look like when it was 12...or when it was 28.

This information isn't intended to answer every question, for there are some we can only speculate on at the present. But what we have said is not speculation. We are dealing in certainties when we say:

- The child you lost now has a human physical form, and is not an airy ghost floating somewhere in space.
- You will meet him or her some day, and will simply and immediately "know" who they are, for we will be in the era where "we will know as we are known." [3]
- The physical form is as unpredictable to you now as it was before birth, but is very possibly like the body his or her genetic code would have dictated had the child lived.

God's Word is amazing, isn't it!
Just like His grace.

NOTES
1. 2 Samuel 12:19-23
2. Psalm 139:16
3. See 1 Corinthians 13:9-12

6
Instruments of Healing

All truth is for action,
not merely for meditation.

THE STATEMENTS ON THE PREVIOUS PAGES ARE
consistent with biblical revelation.

We aren't guessing.

And in the light of all we have discovered,
the question naturally should occur: What
should I do about all of this? All truth is for
action, not merely for meditation. Because God
reveals His will in His Word to direct us, not
merely to inform us, His Word is designed to
assist us to a response that aligns us with His
will. One certainty is that He wants us all to
become instruments of love, His life and His
healing, and I want to invite you to take some
steps forward along that pathway.

Understanding the *Truth* About God

The truths we've studied have to do with the
removal of the confusion surrounding the destiny of the unborn or newly born who are lost
through death. The Word shows their significance, purpose and eternal potential, and
holds forth the certainty that these children
shall have physical forms in the world to come.
The Bible offers the prospect of a new world, a
new togetherness, a new dimension of relationship.

There is a verse of Scripture that is often
quoted, and it's amazing what we have done

with it! We clip off the beginning and forget the end. We quote: "All things work together for good." And half of the time, the verse is quoted with a *que sera sera* attitude; a passive stance that suggests "what will be, will be," as though we are helpless victims of God's sovereign will who, whatever happens, just have to hope for the best.

But that's not what this verse says. There's a certainty in it: "*And we know that all things work together for good to those who love God, to those who are the called according to His purpose.*"[1] What the passage is really saying is that no matter how our soul's enemy attacks or human circumstances impact our lives, God can ultimately take the pain or problem, redeem it and use it for our good. What Satan planned for evil, God can turn for good.

It's possible that coping with the loss of your child has led you down a path of bitterness and anger.

But your loss wasn't God's fault. We live in a broken, imperfect world and we are members of a fallen race. The residual fallout of that fall continually appears around us in the form of sickness, sin, natural disaster, tragedy and death. If, however, you make God the focus of your frustration, you not only fail to receive the comfort He can give, but you are wasting emotional energy aiming your anger at the wrong target.

Embrace the Process of Grief

The attitude of many bystanders toward the loss of a child through miscarriage, abortion, stillbirth or death shortly after birth can sometimes verge on outright insensitivity. You probably know the kind of people I'm talking about. These people may have responded to your child as almost a nonentity, particularly if the child died in the womb before you had a chance to actually physically hold and touch that new little life. These same people may have downplayed your grief, leading you to feel almost abnormal for experiencing deep grief and a sense of loss for the baby you never really got to know.

Please be comforted. Just as Scripture has evidenced the reality and significance of the life once nurtured in your womb, your loss is also real and significant. Don't be surprised if you experience the same general cycle of grief as anyone who has lost a loved one. Indeed, the depth of feeling may not be as great or the season of grief as prolonged, because there are few, if any, memories to deal with. But so often there are *dreams* that became unfulfilled;

anticipated *joy* that was suddenly quenched.

Are you among those who, as soon as you found out about your pregnancy, your heart began to grow to love and encompass that new little life? Though you didn't know your child, did his or her "early flight" leave a vacuum in your heart? Let none of us ever be surprised or embarrassed by such deep emotions over the passing of a fetus. The loss is a real one. And when grief is present, it needs to be accepted, acknowledged and responded to.

But there's another problem to face. Often we feel that if we've effectively pushed our emotions into some kind of submission that we've dealt with everything. Conquering feelings of pain or denying the reality of the depth of mourning through stoical denial of genuine human emotions can leave us emotionally desolate—or worse. And anger left undealt with can quickly turn into bitterness. Furthermore, people are often bewildered by completely false ideas and speak of God having "taken the child from them." How often it is suggested that God "took back" the life He had earlier "given from heaven." But this unscriptural idea is no more true for having been so frequently parroted, or so poetically spoken at the funerals of young children. However well-intended, such misguided words both miss the mark of truth and build walls of fear. You may say, "If God took my child, how can I trust Him with my own life? Why should I trust a God who cares so little for my deepest, most fragile needs and emotions?" But listen, loved ones. God didn't and doesn't "take babies because He needs them in heaven."

So allow understanding to enter your soul. If you recognize anger over the loss of your child, deal with it now. The capacity of the human mind to go down its dead-end labyrinthine ways is amazing. We may think that suppression will help us overcome the pain, but it never does. Grief often includes submerged feelings of either fear or anger. They *can* be dealt with, and here's how.

A major dynamic in the process of working through one's grief is found in the simple act of talking—to God, to family and to friends in your support system.

We need to talk to each other. One of the greatest lies our soul's enemy conjures is that what concerns you isn't worth anybody else's time. Or that the only place you can turn is to someone that you pay to listen—a psychiatrist, doctor or pastor. While these professionals may be very helpful, and certainly have their place, be sure to allow your family, friends, and church fellowship to help you work through the hard times related to your loss.

Begin with prayer.

I mean, just talk to God.

Talk with the Lord about the child you once had. Openly describe your bewilderment, your questions. Believe in His loving willingness to embrace you in your pain—and even to understand your fears. But, dear friend, don't *blame* Him. Trust Him.

Further, if you feel the desire to do so, express your heart of love toward your child. Do it before God. While we know that communicating with a loved one is *not* possible (and attempting to do so opens a person to being deceived by Satan), we *can* talk freely with God about all our feelings, discussing any questions our hearts want to ask. But remember, if you have felt any anger toward God, let these truths we've covered bring a change of mind. He knows our hearts and not only forgives our misunderstandings, but as the one perfect, loving Father, He welcomes our coming to Him—even spilling out our tears, our sorrow or our heartache. Bring it all into His presence. He not only will accept your heart cry, *He will comfort you.*

Let any heartbreak open the door to discovering God's infinite mercy, His gentleness and His graciousness. He's the Redeemer, and His loving kindness and mercy are past finding out. I encourage you to talk with "Abba"—that's the Hebrew word for "Daddy." His Holy Spirit wants to help you do that—and He's the best Comforter of all.[2]

Remember, too, that God promises a reunion someday with your child. *Meaning* comes to the miscarrying mother: "I may not have been able to receive my child now, but my pregnancy was not a waste of time." *Hope* comes to the parents of stillborn or those who died early in infancy: "We never got a chance to know you...but we shall, some day." And for the mother who chose an abortion, there is *peace*: "One day we will meet again in heaven, where our relationship will be whole and restored." In the light of that meaning, hope and peace God gives, it is perfectly proper to say, "I'll hold you in heaven." There will be a day of meeting that child.

In 1 Thessalonians 4, the apostle Paul examined the implications of the coming of Christ, helping people understand how the dead will be resurrected at Jesus' coming. He helped them come to an understanding of how the living and the dead who are prepared through a relationship with God will be gathered together in one grand and mighty reunion. It was in this content that he told them, "Comfort one another with these words...we will always be with the Lord."[3] At that time of our being eternally gathered unto the Living God who made us, we shall forever be with Him—*and* with one another. It's not a dream, a myth or a humanly concocted fable. Our real and resurrected Savior, Jesus Christ, has promised this to all who trust in Him, and we can count on it. He's the fulness of Truth—the Son of God!

Put Guilt in Its Place

I'm convinced that guilt is a natural part of the grief cycle. It's the human response of trying to find a logical, explainable answer for every tragedy. Yet the ramifications of unresolved guilt are profound, resulting in:

- shaken assurance, as we begin to doubt the very foundations upon which our life is built;
- crippled confidence, as we move through each day with foggy uncertainty, often unable to deal with the demands those days bring and;
- fragile faith, as we begin to wonder if or how God fits into life's harsh realities.

But God has a remedy for all these symptoms guilt produces. He calls us to *confront* guilt—to put it in its place. He doesn't require this for the purpose of reopening a wound, but rather to allow us to deal conclusively with any condemnation or doubt we may feel that we might find freedom from it. You see, when our emotions are vulnerable, the Adversary—Satan—preys on our pain, clawing those raw emotions with guilt or condemnation. Particularly in the wake of a death, feelings of unfounded guilt may abound.

For example, I remember how my own son-in-law was racked by guilt over the death of his brother in a tragic accident, because he had missed praying for him that day. Listen, loved one. Rest your guilt-driven grief on God's grace. Please, in Jesus' name, lay aside those feelings of guilt.

Sometimes, however, a portion of the guilt is founded. I can't deny the existence—and necessity—of the healthy dynamic of this guilt, for I have met too many who, through it, found relief. Some, stricken with the remorse and grief over their decision to carry through the act of abortion, have been right to acknowledge their sorry failure, and even *more* righteous to bring it humbly to our loving, forgiving Father God. If this is the case with your heart, it's important to let the guilt do its job, bringing you to repentance. Cleansing and full forgiveness will fully follow, for there is no decision or choice we could have made that's powerful enough to keep us from the cleansing, healing power of God's grace in Jesus Christ.

Come to Him.

And once your relationship with God is restored, your guilt has served its purpose and no longer has any place in your life.

Let it go. And refuse its argument to regain any place in tormenting your mind or your feelings.

Being rid of guilt—either imagined or real guilt that has been resolved through the blood of Jesus Christ—is, however, sometimes easier described than done. But listen! God Himself has provided the means by which we can launch and sustain a victory over guilt. By the prophet Isaiah, God commanded, "Sing and shout because of what I've done. I have redeemed, I have blotted out, so sing and shout."[4] God's Word says it simply: Sing. Why not do it *now*. Quietly, as you sit where you are—at least hum,

> *Amazing grace, how sweet the sound,*
> *That saved a wretch like me.*
> *I once was lost but now am found;*
> *Was blind and now I see.*[5]

When you begin to sing, praise God thankfully, rather than trying to reason everything out. His Holy Spirit will begin loosening any chains that seem to bind you to feelings of guilt.

And if the arch-liar persists in plaguing you with any further condemnation, simply rest your case on the presence of God's Living Word:

> *So there is now no condemnation awaiting those who belong to Christ Jesus. For the power of the life-giving Spirit—and this power is mine through Christ Jesus— has freed me from the vicious circle of sin and death.*[6]

NOTES
1. Romans 8:28
2. Galatians 4:6; John 14:15-18
3. 1 Thessalonians 4:15-18
4. Isaiah 44:22,23 (author's paraphrase)
5. John Newton, "Amazing Grace." Public domain.
6. Romans 8:1,2 *The Living Bible*

7

The Heartbeat
of Love

This is My body,
which is broken for you.

—1 Corinthians 11:24

A S WE FIND PRACTICAL STEPS TO TAKE THROUGH OUR studying the truth of God's Word, let's proceed to another level of need. What can we do to help stanch the flow of lost lives and lost hope resulting from abortion?

There are attitudes to be assessed and actions to take, and the heartbeat of both is in one word: *Love.* Love that reaches with life to cast out fear.

A great many people today have deep feelings about abortion; feelings that tug, anger, pinch and strangle. But I wish everyone who has ever been concerned about or scarred by abortion could have been there that morning. What happened, right in the middle of a worship service with several thousand people present would, I think, affect anyone's thinking. That morning everyone felt good about *not* having abortions—but no one felt smug, self-righteous or superior for having this feeling.

Here's the story.

I'll call her Tammy, to protect her real identity. She wasn't a girl without sexual values, but neither did her life have a spiritual base. Some months into her new city experience and her new job, Tammy met a nice fellow. They began to date and, not because either were generally promiscuous, but because they were simply human, and because neither had any personal spiritual experience, strength or guidance to help anything be otherwise, Tammy and her boyfriend had intercourse—and Tammy got pregnant.

He ran.

Yep, her boyfriend was scared.

That might not be a very noble response on his part, but before you go too hard on the boy, remember what we're talking about: Two young people, hardly even adults in some respects, though in their early twenties, without spiritual roots, carried away by emotion. Well, this fellow was anything but ready for a family, so he ran.

But Tammy couldn't run.

The problem was inside her body. And what was only as yet a small mass of cells multiplying at a phenomenal rate every day, brought terrifying fear to the girl.

She was new to the city, new to her work environment, newly in love—at least she had thought so. And now she was about to become a new parent—and without a partner.

Tammy wrestled with the plaguing fears. She called her parents and they immediately and completely rejected her, offering nothing of support, guidance or counsel except, "Don't come home." It was then she decided to check the Yellow Pages for some place she might inquire into an abortion.

The previous edition of those same pages, until the new phone book had come out one month before, was much the same as in most cities of our nation. Dozens of abortion clinics were listed—veiled with names that suggest counsel and consultation, but which usually advise "Abort."

Occasionally an alternative point of counsel was available (in this book there was one). But even then it was not from a Christian perspective—that is, not with the patient wisdom and gentle power in the touch the Spirit of God brings to any human need.

But, as I said, a *new* phone book had just been published—and for the first time in more than a dozen years since the Supreme Court's infamous Roe v. Wade decision, which brought on the wholesale practice of abortion in the United States, this phone book had a number to call that offered something different. There was an ad—picture of one hand reaching for another, with the words—"Touchpoint—Free Pregnancy Testing...Immediate Results—Referrals offered."

And Tammy called.

What Tammy didn't know is the number she called reached a phone in an office opened only days before; opened because one church caught a vision and thousands of its members believed in it enough to give the funds needed to launch its fulfillment.

The vision was this:

- To provide a point of reference for pregnancy counselling without imposing a spiritual demand on the inquirer; but distinctly discouraging abortion—and providing options.
- To trust the Holy Spirit to bless the counselees by causing their hearts to open to the gentle understanding shown.
- That by this process, lives would be touched, women ministered to and babies saved.

And Tammy had called—which leads back to the worship service I mentioned taking place that special morning; the special day that Tammy came to church with her baby.

You see, following that phone call, a lot of time, a lot of patience and a gracious, unpressuring influence had been shown and given to Tammy. She immediately recognized a quality of life—of love—she'd never known before. The result is that Tammy decided against abortion, a little while later received Jesus Christ as her Savior, and on this special Sunday had brought her newborn baby girl for dedication to the Lord.

Although there was no baby's daddy or husband present beside Tammy, elders from this congregation stood with their wives beside the young woman, and the pastor briefly told her story—having been given Tammy's permission to do so.

Preparing to take Communion, everyone in the room held in hand the broken bread, over which Jesus spoke saying, *"This is My body, broken for you...."* [1] The pastor spoke about the intent of Christ, that through His brokenness a wholeness be ministered to mankind, and at that point invited Tammy and the baby to come to the platform.

The worshipers, though not used to such an interruption at the Lord's Table, listened with tear-moistened eyes as Tammy's story was related. Then the pastor took the baby in his arms and said: "This is as dramatic a case as I think you'll ever see, in which brokenness is made whole through the love of Jesus. This baby would have been broken in the womb, but it wasn't. Because you prayed, you gave and you loved, Tammy found new possibilities, and here in my arms is wholeness, not brokenness."

It was an incredible morning, and all the more wonderful when, shortly after that service, a phone call to Tammy's parents found a changed attitude on their part. Their hearts had been touched that someone, somewhere had helped their daughter in her personal crisis. Now they wanted to do their part.

Today, Tammy is home having been lovingly welcomed there by her folks who are helping their daughter forward in life—with their little grandchild as well.

You'll pardon me if I seem to relate this in a slightly emotional way, because I was there.

I was the pastor.

Ours was the congregation.

I held that baby in my arms and presented it before Father God in the rite of dedication. But the reason I was moved was not simply because a baby's life was spared; it was because the event itself would never have happened had not something else occurred.

It involved three very large steps in a change of attitude. In relating them to you, I risk being badly misunderstood, but I've decided to run that risk. Too many lives are at stake for smallness on my part to prompt hesitation; or, for that matter smallness on any of our part. Because I think there is a smallness in many of us not produced by a willful stinginess of soul so much as by the fear to love.

Let me describe the starting place I was at, and from which those three steps brought me and those who walked that path with me. They brought us, in the end, to a larger place of service and a greater ministering of Jesus' love.

NOTE
1. 1 Corinthians 11:24

8

Three Steps to Loving

For God demonstrates His own love toward us, in that while we were still sinners, Christ died for us.

—Romans 5:8

Responding Emotionally: Overcoming Self-Righteousness

In one way or another all of us are people walking through a living graveyard.

Everywhere we go, among everyone we meet every day, there are the walking dead. They are people so radically impacted by death in one way or another that they are not only candidates for *healing*—they need a resurrection. Death has come to them in one or more of a hundred forms. There isn't anyone you'll meet today that hasn't been touched by it:

- the death of relationships,
- the death of dreams,
- the death of a business enterprise,
- the death of a loved one.

These aren't negative observations made by one who views life dismally. I'm simply noting the fact that death is present in many, many ways. And you and I have been prepared to bring a living answer!

But before that can happen, many of us need a melting of our hearts. I know I did— and a number of factors contributed to God's bringing it about. It began with an ulterior viewpoint on a self-righteousness I didn't see in my own attitudes.

I knew the Word of God and I knew abortion was wrong: I opposed it, prayed for people who practiced it, and prayed against its spread in our nation. And I sometimes got mad when I would see television news reports displaying the militant actions of so called "pro-choice" advocates. But as I said earlier, God radically changed my attitude without changing my convictions.

For example, I had never had to deal with the victim of forcible incest or rape—a woman pregnant with a baby produced by an involuntary or violent act. Nor had I ever thought much about the agony of soul in a woman whose child within was known already to be deformed. Nor had I considered the emotional plight of the husband whose wife's own health was imperiled to the point that she would probably bear the child at the expense of her life.

Rape.

Incest.

Known deformity in the womb.

Mother's health.

These were issues I had hardly considered. For my part, I was not ready to concede that abortion was the answer to any of these situations. And I must gently say that I'm still not. But at the same time, I have had to come to the point that I not only can, I simply must allow for the price of *fear*—yes, even *selfishness* if anyone may judge it to be so—when someone chooses an abortion in any such situations.

Listen.

Listen, please. I make such allowance not because I believe it may necessarily be the right choice, but because all of us, as fallible human beings, have all made wrong choices! And when I see someone who has made a wrong choice—even in the face of alternative counseling that I have given—I cannot, in the Spirit of Christ, sit in judgment on them for that.

As a fallible, sinning human being I, too, have felt fear that has begotten actions less than worthy or faith-filled. And now, suddenly, I was being shaken by God's Word at the very point at which my self-righteousness toward abortion had been so conveniently sustained. I was being confronted by the Holy Spirit; being reminded that I was to love exactly as He loves.

> *But God demonstrates His own love toward us, in that while we were still sinners, Christ died for us.*[1]

Of course, I knew that verse before, but I had always applied it to the doctrine of God's salvation, and not seen it as the duty of a Christian. In other words, I could see how necessary it was that God loved me first, in order to reach me with His love. Beyond my blindness to His way, my ignorance of His will, my indifference to His Spirit, and in spite of my self-serving sinfulness, His love was unconditional. His Word is marvelously clear and the truth incredibly freeing: His love is unbounded, unending and fully offered *in advance.*

But I'd never had it settle upon my soul that He was calling me to love people the same way He does. My evangelical orthodoxy required me to insist that I had to overcome sin by resisting it in others—not only in myself. Wherever I found it, I found myself succumbing to a "watchdog" mentality of critiquing my culture, rather than a shepherd mindset toward lovingly seeking the lost. That is, until I thought through the way Jesus overcame sin. The way He overcame sin was in surrendering Himself to love—to stand forgivingly before it until His love overcame it.

Now I was being forced to confront this fact: God wanted me to love people who had abortions, whether I agreed or not. And He wanted me to do it without the usual verbal appendage, "Okay, I'll love them, but I still hate their sin."

I think we may too easily employ that ruse

to satisfy our emotional outrage, and when we do, the hatred too often spills over and poisons our best efforts at serving the lost. Can you imagine Jesus on the cross saying, "Father, forgive them, they don't know what they're doing..and I hate it. I can't say how *much* I hate it, but I'll still love them, though I assure you I hate their sin."

Oh, don't make any mistake. Don't think I'm soft on sin, nor am I arguing that God is.

Never.

The reason Christ *died* for sin is that sin is deadly serious business, and the death-price has to be paid in full, one way or the other. When we take matters into our own hands, death prevails. But when we trust what His almighty power has accomplished in *His* dying, life can win!

I was beginning to realize that my unloving attitude was not a necessary ingredient to insure a sufficient payment for people's sins. God didn't need me to be mad at their sin—to hate it—in order to assure it was fully compensated for. He had only commissioned me to be a reconciler—to help people be reconciled to Him by reaching with His love, understanding and tenderness.[2] When I came to terms with the fact that a lot of people aborting children were no less or no more sinful than I was, I found I was far more ready to understand the fears, emotion and torment of a woman facing a pregnancy she feared or didn't want. I *wasn't* any more ready to agree she should terminate it, but I *was* more ready to accept the person who made that decision.

Responding Intellectually: Surveying the Potential for Disaster

I was now ready to do something about it. And something does need to be done.

The painful matter of abortion cannot interminably go on being condemned by the indignant while it is promoted by its proponents. The issue isn't only that life's possibilities are being removed from the millions affected, it has to do with attitudes toward the *control* of life; life as it concerns *all of us*—the billions on this planet right now.

Thoughtful analysis of the moral question concerning abortion and those who propose that "on demand" privilege be outlawed, are not simplistically pontificating a pro-life cause. They are forcing us to look at the drift set in motion once a society accepts the privilege of terminating *any* human life at will *and* with impunity.

Where does the process stop?

If life is disallowed in the womb on the front end of its span, what is to stop the evolution of a social policy that may at will, any time and with impunity, stop it on the other end? If we can legally take a baby's life in the womb, will the next step be taking grandpa's life when he's old; exterminating him as a willful act simply because he's more an inconvenience than a contribution to the community? ("After all, he isn't doing well anyway.")

And then euthanasia. "Mercy killing," they call it.

When suffering intensifies, and the agony of the family looking on is only exceeded by the agony of a loved one in the throes of death as violent disease and indescribable torturous pain rack an aging body, what then?

Who should play God?

That question probes our social consciousness, and people who think abortion is but a single issue need to look into the extended ramifications of its acceptance.

Further, this doesn't even begin to explore the implications of genetic engineering and alternative approaches to conception and childbearing. Who can forecast the long-range effect of present research and activity in genetic manipulation, recombinant DNA, extra-uterine conception, surrogate motherhood, sperm banks and the experimentation of cloning?

I'm not ready to prophesy the birth of a troop of Frankenstein monsters, but neither can I retire to an ostrich-like stance of passivity, pretending that present trends are only passing fads. Man is dabbling in the *control* of life, not merely its reproduction, and there is no scriptural indication that his God-given assignment to "subdue" the earth and "replenish it" even includes much of what he's into right now.

I'm certainly not resistant to the scientific research that has often blessed mankind with benevolent results. But I don't think we can neglect the fact that there are some very negative implications in some of what is happening. Social ethics are spiritual issues, and they are being dramatically impacted by today's applied biological research.

Responding Spiritually: Getting Involved

I recently appealed to our congregation to do something to indicate our interest in the life of the unborn child. I wasn't proposing a march on city hall; I didn't offer placards or design a sit-in at a clinic. And I certainly DID make clear my revulsion at the hideous actions of people who bomb clinics in that insane expression of protest. But I further said, "We can't do *nothing.*"

Following that Sunday, I received a letter from a man who I think expresses what some Christians suppose to be a spiritual response: "I don't think the Church should be involved in political issues," he wrote.

I could hardly believe my eyes: *A political issue?!*

We were talking about LIFE.

We were talking about morality.

We were talking about loving people who are afraid to accept the life conceived within them, and trying to lovingly serve them amid those fears.

However well-intended or supposedly spiritual his motivation, this man reflected the fact that in all of us there is the temptation to find some escape from responsibility for action. I know I would rather leave it all alone; the subject bothers me. But I had to listen to Proverbs 31:8,9.

> *Open your mouth for the speechless, in the cause of all who are appointed to die. Open your mouth, judge righteously, and plead the cause of the poor and needy.*

I had (1) faced the facts of my self-righteousness, (2) broadened my perspective on what was happening in some people facing tough situations, and (3) now had taken a hard look at social and moral questions facing us today. But with the third step, what could I do?

Well, I'm not a very political, protest-type person. In fact, I have difficulty with the idea of "The Church" marching in any arena other than on its knees. I'm sure my feelings wouldn't seem tough enough to satisfy a lot of good Christians, while others would doubtless assess my position as being "too strict."

But I did arrive at a point of action that somehow strikes me as one balanced between judgment and mercy. It involves:

- Ministering *personally* in the spirit and the truth I've presented in this book; and,
- Ministering *publicly* by serving people in our society with a living option, through providing the type of resource that resulted in the rescue of Tammy's baby.

The addendum that follows may be utilized as you, or any church leader you have contact with, may wish to pursue. For me it accomplished the third step in *loving*. I hope it might help you do the same.

There *is* a turnaround taking place in the thought and actions of many today. I know, because of a massive surge of God's grace that helped me "turn"—to rethink the problems of just one arena of pain tormenting people like you and me.

I hope this chronicle of my journey, self-discovery and the ensuing truth-discoveries in God's Word, make a full circle possible. May you know Christ's healing and fullness, and may you become a transmitter of His life.

With a heart full of His love and forgiveness, let us each be instant to obey and constant in doing what the angel commended long ago: *"Go...and speak to the people all the words of this life."* [3]

NOTES
1. Romans 5:8
2. 2 Corinthians 5:18-21
3. Acts 5:20

Addendum

I have asked a friend, Geoff Thompson, who developed and launched one church's Crisis Pregnancy Center, to write a few words of practical guidance. This guide is for any group of believers looking for an effective, confrontive, loving and serving answer to the social crisis of "abortion on demand."

But, intercessory prayer is the master key to any transformation in individuals or societies. Geoff has given this information with the understanding that prayer, prayer, and more prayer must precede and accompany any effort. All that we do in seeking to reach, touch and change our world is "Not by might nor by power but by My Spirit' says the Lord of hosts." [1]

Franky Schaeffer has said that every Christian should picket an abortion clinic. I understand his statement and his sentiments. In 1941, the German people allowed millions of

Jews to be hauled off because in the late 1930s, they allowed the Jews to be called *Untermenschen* or "less than people." For us to do nothing against the wholesale slaughter of the innocent would be unthinkable.

But picketing isn't the only way. Sidewalk counselling—approaching women before they enter an abortion clinic and lovingly informing them about other choices—is often successful in changing a woman's mind. Forming a "speakers bureau" to address local high schools and colleges brings the message of life and hope to hundreds.

One of the best ways to touch mothers, fathers and the as-yet-unborn babies is through a Crisis Pregnancy Center.

Every abortion takes a number of victims. The woman is often confused, pressured and deceived, frequently facing lasting physical and psychological consequences. In Isaiah 49:15, God asks, "Can a woman forget her nursing child, and not have compassion on the son of her womb?" A woman cannot abort her unborn child without suffering the consequences. A Crisis Pregnancy Center can focus on the woman and her needs, and offer her acceptance, compassion and accurate information about abortion and the alternatives.

The Center can also minister to the father,

who may have all the same emotions as the mother, and extend the love of Christ to him, offering forgiveness as well as practical options and wise counsel that will allow his future to be hopeful, rather than hateful.

Through these extensions of love and guidance, the unborn baby is given a chance at life. God calls His people to rescue those being led away to death, to hold back those staggering toward slaughter.[2] Through care and concern with the parents who can communicate, we may be able to save the life of a child who can't.

How to Start a Crisis Pregnancy Center

1. Form a Steering Committee From its inception, a CPC should be developed under the leadership of several persons who represent a wide range of Bible-believing Christians. Proverbs 15:22 states that "Without counsel, plans go awry, but in the multitude of counselors they are established."

2. Contact the Christian Action Council Since 1975, when it was begun in the home of Billy Graham, the CAC has become the largest Christian organization of its kind, committed to help ministries begin Crisis Pregnancy Centers. With local chapters or constituents in all 50 states and most provinces in Canada, the CAC will assist the development of, and training for a viable CPC (101 W. Broad Street, Suite 500, Falls Church, VA 22046; 703-237-2100).

3. Complete a Community Survey Using the resources of the CAC, and the manpower of the Steering Committee, take a survey of your community. This information will help to identify the need for a CPC and pinpoint the public and private facilities that are already available.

4. Incorporate and Elect a Board of Directors Under a nonprofit heading, funds can be raised for the ministry. Consequently, the limit of liability and the individuality of the ministry remain separate from any church.

5. Establish Working Committees Within the Board Once the Board of Directors has been established, divide the work into separate committees: Public Relations, Finance Fund-raising, Facility Location, Training, Shepherding Homes, Volunteers.

6. *Hire a Director* The CPC must *compete* with a professional quality and attitude of excellence that is equal to or greater than other abortion clinics. For this reason alone, a director is needed; not only to oversee the operation, but to provide supervision to volunteers. Because this is a spiritual outreach as well as a professional one, the center needs the covering and leadership that a Christian servant can provide.

7. *Train Volunteers* The CAC provides hours of intensive training and materials to help your center get off the ground.

Obviously these steps are neither exclusive nor comprehensive. They do, however, highlight the fact that if God calls you to reach out into your community with the light of hope and the life of Christ, given a vision to do so, you could be just months away from a Crisis Pregnancy Center.

———
NOTES
1. Zechariah 4:6
2. See Proverbs 24:11,12

To Complement and Supplement Your Reading

AUDIOCASSETTE TAPES...

...of related teachings by Pastor Hayford are available through the SoundWord Tape Ministry for $5.00 each. The following list suggests messages that correlate closely with the theme of *I'll Hold You In Heaven.*

TITLE	ITEM NUMBER
"Short-circuited into Eternity"	#1335
"Abortion and Adoption"	#1521
"Why People Sometimes Die too Soon"	#1451
"Testimony of Triumph"	# 354

A SoundWord Tape Catalog is available for $2.00 ($3.00 outside the United States). This attractive catalog features more than 70 pages of teaching resources by Pastor Hayford. It covers exegetical Bible studies and practical topics geared to "equip the saints for the work of the ministry."

New believers, as well as seasoned pastors, will find listings for more than 3,000 audiotapes, along with scores of videotapes for home and group use from the SoundWord Tape Ministry. In addition, you may select resources from the wide selection of many books, booklets, and pamphlets by Pastor Hayford.

> Please write to:
> Living Way Ministries
> Resource Department
> 14480 Sherman Way
> Van Nuys, CA 91405-2396

Resources may also be ordered by credit card by calling 1-800-776-8180, Tuesday through Friday, 9:00 A.M. to 5:00 P.M. (PST).

✂ ————————————— remove here —————————————

Dear Jack,

I have read *I'll Hold You in Heaven*, and while doing so came to the time and place where I have made my decision to receive the Lord Jesus Christ as my personal Savior.

I would appreciate it if you would send me the gift copy of *NEWBORN: Your New Life in Christ*, as I begin life with Him.

Please mail to:

Your name _____

Address _____

City _____ State _____ Zip _____

NEWBORN will
be sent to you
free of charge.

Mail this request to:
Dr. Jack Hayford
The Church On The Way (LWM)
14800 Sherman Way
Van Nuys, CA 91405